STRINGSTASTIC
Level 3

By Lorraine Chai
2nd Edition

PO BOX 815 Epping NSW 1710 Australia
www.stringstastic.com
Copyright © 2019 Lorraine Chai
First Published 2019
2nd Edition 2020
USA Edition 2021

Book design by Meilisa Lengkong

All rights reserved.
Reproduction in whole or in part for any use whatsoever is strictly prohibited.

THE AUTHOR
LORRAINE CHAI

Lorraine is a multi-talented instrumentalist and an international educator. She graduated from the Sydney Conservatorium of Music with a Bachelor of Music Studies in 2008 and completed her Graduate Diploma of Education at the Australian Catholic University a year later.

Having grown up in a musical family, Lorraine began piano lessons at the age of four and violin at the age of six, giving her first violin performance at just seven years of age. Lorraine started teaching violin at the age of 14 and founded a string ensemble at her local church. From there, teaching and performing became her passion.

Lorraine loves finding new and exciting ways students can learn their instrument in a classroom setting as well as in private lessons. Along with her musical journey and exposure to the various educational methods including Kodaly, Suzuki, Orff, and Dalcroze, Lorraine has also attended Alexander Technique workshops and has found that she can integrate these various methods into her own teaching technique for the benefit of her students.

Lorraine has extensive ensemble and orchestral experience in Malaysia and in Australia. Lorraine is currently the Music Director of Stringstastic Pty Ltd and is an active member of the Australian Strings Association, AUSTA NSW. She also co-ordinates instrumental programmes and runs string ensembles for some of Sydney's most celebrated schools.

PREFACE

Stringstastic cello Level 3 follows from the knowledge that young players have gained in Stringstastic cello Level 1 and Level 2. Stringstastic cello Level 3 extends that knowledge through games and fun graphics to assist young beginner cellists to help them better understanding the instrument and learn music theory in an enjoyable way. This Stringstastic series can be used in a private lesson or alongside the violin, viola, and double bass book series in a classroom setting.

For extra resources, go to www.stringstastic.com to download them for free.

Have fun!!

ACKNOWLEDGEMENT

This book was made possible with the encouragement of my family and loved ones. I would like to thank the following for their advice and input in making this book possible.

Dr. Rita Crews OAM, FMusA (honoris causa), PhD(UNE), BA(Hons), AMusTCL, GradCertDistEd (UNE), FMusicolASMC, HonFNMSM, DipMus (honoris causa) (AICM) MIMT, MACE, MMTA, JP.

Mary Nemet AMusA, is a prominent string educator, AMEB Examiner, Reviews Editor for AUSTA Stringendo and contributor to Strings USA.

Helen Tuckey PG Dip Music (Manhattan School of Music), AMusA, MIMT, DipArts(music) (Victorian College of the Arts)

David Pereira DSCM, MMus (Indiana University)

CONTENTS

4	REVISION
7	NOTE AND REST VALUES
11	NEW TIME SIGNATURE
15	READING RHYTHMS
18	RELATIVE MINORS AND MAJORS
21	MINOR SCALES
26	MINOR ARPEGGIOS
28	LABELLING SCALES AND ARPEGGIOS
29	WHAT HAVE WE LEARNT SO FAR?
31	SEQUENCES
32	OSTINATO
33	ITALIAN TERMS
35	COMPOSITION
37	ANACRUSIS
39	HALF POSITION
40	FORWARD EXTENSION
42	LAST REVISION
44	TEST

STRINGSTASTIC

Revision

Let us revise naming the notes on the bass clef. A reminder that we only use the first 7 letters of the alphabet. After G the note goes back to A.

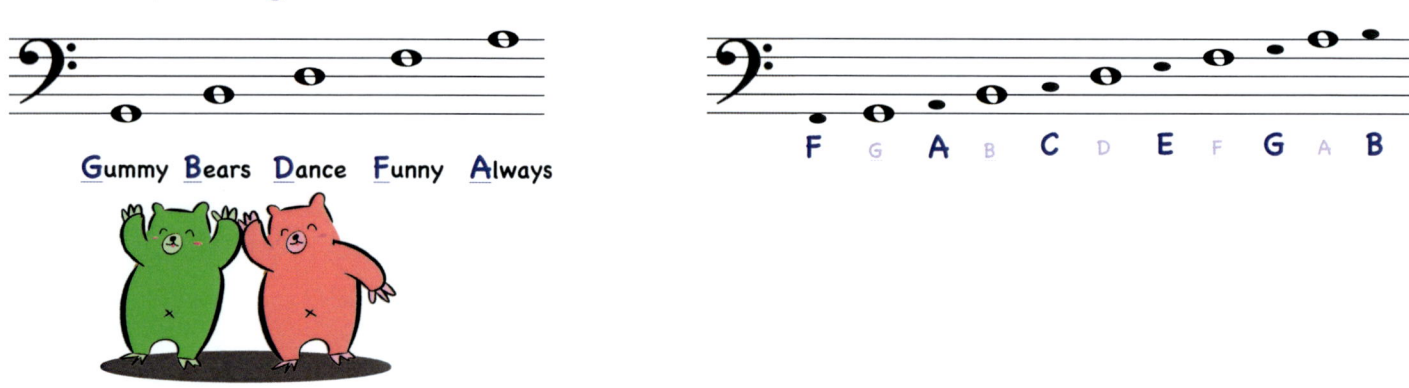

Name these notes without looking back to the top of the page.
(**REMINDER**: Use capital letters.)

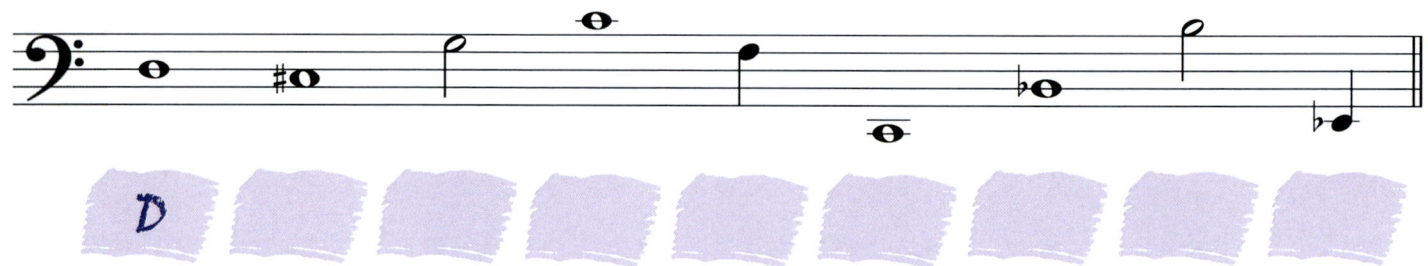

In first position, write out the fingering above the notes in the question above.
(Refer to page 39 for explanation of the different positions on the instrument.)

Name the string where each of these notes can be found.
(**REMINDER**: Careful with the fingering.)

	Note	String
①③④	F	C String
①②④	B♭	
①③④	G	
①②④	E♭	
①③④	B	

	Note	String
①③④	A	
①③④	D	
①②④	C	
①③④	C	
①②④	F	

In semibreve notes, draw **THREE** different C sharps.

Eg.
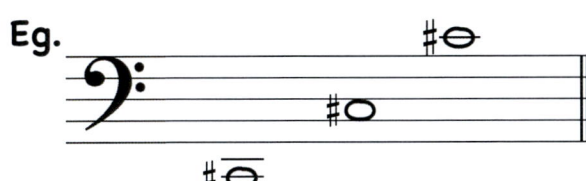

In crotchet notes, draw **THREE** different C naturals.

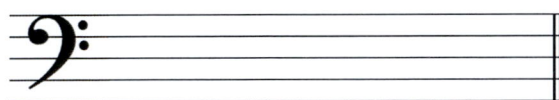

Reminder:
ledger lines are drawn the same distance away from the staff.

✓

✗ – ledger lines are not the same distance
– floating note

Reminder:
ALWAYS draw the ledger lines first, before the note.

In semibreve notes, draw **THREE** different E flats.

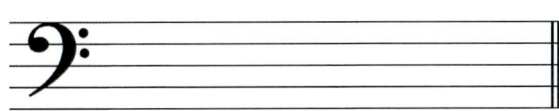

In minim notes, draw **THREE** different D flats.

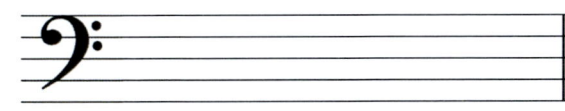

Answer the questions in each square.

a. Draw a note where you use the backward extension (1st finger).
b. Draw the key signature of D major.
c. Place a fermata sign on the note.
d. Show that the next note is a semitone higher.
e. Name the symbol.
f. Name the key signature.
g. Place a tie in a suitable place.
h. Draw 2 quaver notes beamed together.
i. Name this note.
j. Place an accent on this note.
k. Circle the correct italian word that means at a walking pace.
l. Draw a semibreve rest.
m. Show the time signature representing 3 crotchet beats in a bar.
n. Draw a slur over all the notes.
o. What is the value of this rest?

Write out these scales using the correct key signature.
(**REMINDER:** Draw the bass clef.)

<u>D major</u>
 - One octave descending only
 - Use semibreve notes
 - Complete the scale with a double bar line

<u>C major</u>
 - One octave in an ascending and descending order
 - Use minim notes
 - Complete the scale with a double bar line

Note and Rest Values

NAME	NOTE	REST	NOTE VALUE
Semiquaver note	♬ ← double tail	double tail → 𝄿	$1/4$
2 semiquaver notes joined	← beam		$1/4 + 1/4 = 1/2$
4 semiquaver notes joined			1
Dotted crotchet note	♩.		$1\ 1/2$

Instructions for drawing notes.
1. Firstly, draw the note head (seed)
2. Draw the stem (stem of plant)
3. Lastly, draw the tail(s) or beam(s) (leaf)
 - always face the correct side
 - remember 'Pod' or 'Pond'

Draw the tail for each of these notes and rests and write its value.

Semiquaver Note

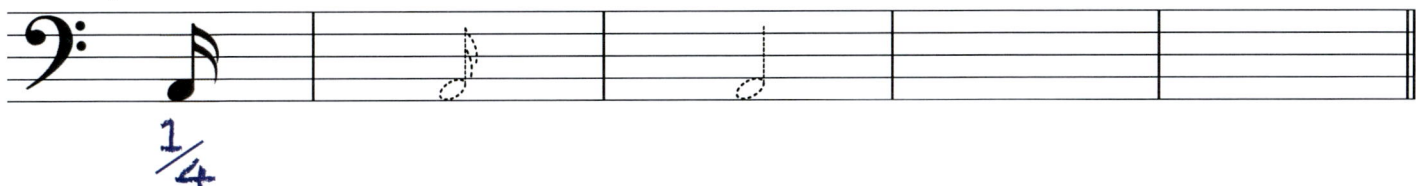

$1/4$

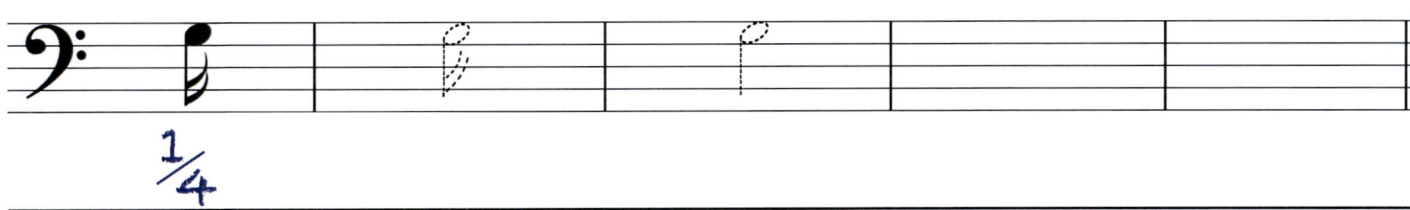

$1/4$

Semiquaver Rest *(draw a dot in the middle 2 spaces)*

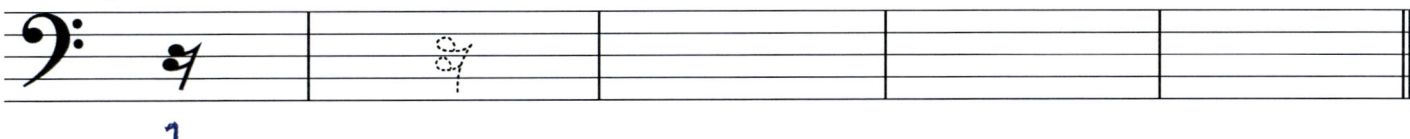

$1/4$

Draw **TWO** semiquavers beamed together.

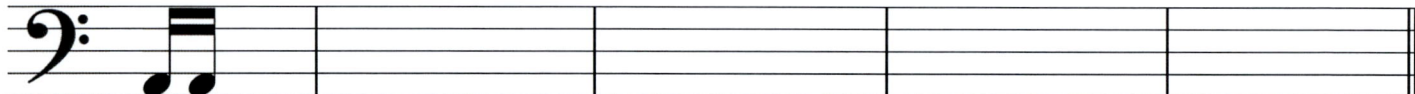

How many crotchet beats are 2 semiquavers worth?

Draw **FOUR** semiquavers beamed together.

How many crotchet beats are 4 semiquavers worth?

A. Figuring out the dotted value.

$\text{𝅗𝅥}\cdot$ = The note itself + ½ value of itself

$$\text{𝅗𝅥} \quad + \quad ½\text{𝅗𝅥}$$

$$2 \quad + \quad 1 \quad = \quad \underline{3}$$

- -

$$\text{♩}\cdot \;=\; \text{♩} \quad + \quad ½\text{♩}$$

$$1 \quad + \quad ½ \quad = \quad \underline{1½}$$

(The dot next to the note means ½ the value of itself.)

B. Quaver note value.

1 quaver = ½ count

2 quavers = 1 count

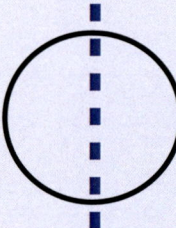

Think of a crotchet as being like a cake or a circle. When we cut it in halves, we have 2 quavers (2 halves of a full cake). When we put them back together, it becomes 1 full circle again.

C. Semiquaver note value.

A semiquaver note has 2 tails and is a smaller note value then a quaver, hence they are quicker notes.

1 semiquaver = $\frac{1}{4}$ count

2 semiquavers = $\frac{1}{2}$ count

4 semiquavers = 1 count

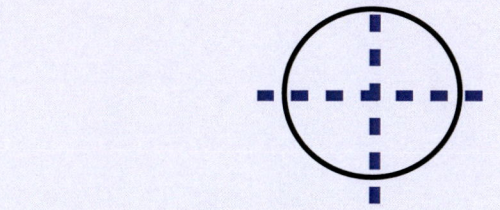

As you can see on the diagram on page 10, we need 4 semiquaver notes to create a crotchet which is a total value of 1 count.

Add the total number of crotchet beats in these note values.

Eg. 3 + ½ = 3 ½ crotchet beats

How many crotchet beats do these notes need to create the same value?

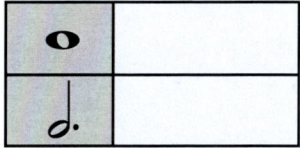

How many quavers beats do these notes need to create the same value?

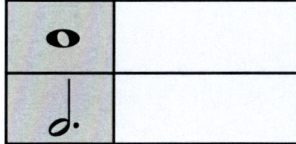

Below is a diagram which shows the number of notes of different lengths which is equal in value to a semibreve.

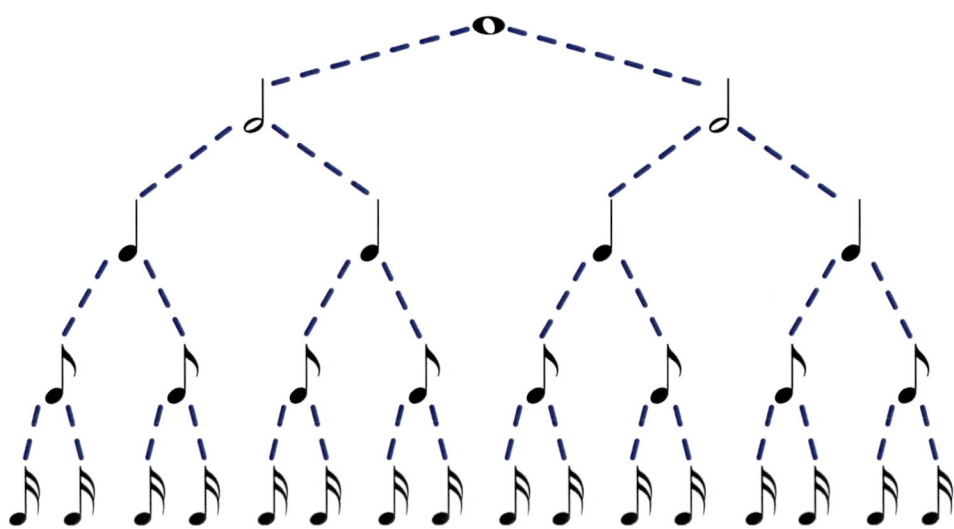

Answer the questions below.

a. How many crotchet beats are there in a semibreve? 4

b. How many quaver beats are there in a minim?

c. How many quaver beats are there in a semibreve?

d. How many crotchet beats are there in a dotted minim?

e. How many semiquaver beats are there in a quaver?

f. How many quaver beats are there in a dotted crotchet?

g. How many semiquaver beats are there in a dotted crotchet?

h. How many semiquaver beats are there in a minim?

i. How many dotted crotchet beats are there in a dotted minim?

j. How many semiquaver beats are there in a semibreve?

k. How many minim beats are there in a semibreve?

l. How many semiquaver beats are there in a minim tied with a quaver?

New Time Signature

The time signature which we have learnt so far has the number 4 at the bottom which shows that we should count in crotchet beats.

$\dfrac{4}{4}$ → number of beats per bar
→ 4 = crotchet beats per bar

In the diagram on page 10, we see that we need 4 crotchet beats to make a semibreve, hence the bottom of the time signature is 4 which shows us that we should count each bar in crotchet beats.

In this book, we will learn to change the number on the bottom of the time signature.

1. $\dfrac{6}{8}$ → looking back at the diagram, we need 8 quavers to make a semibreve. Hence, <u>8 means quaver beats.</u>

$\dfrac{6}{8}$ means there are 6 quaver beats in each bar. The quavers here are grouped in THREEs and beamed together.

When using rests in $\dfrac{6}{8}$, use TWO quaver rests where there are TWO quaver beats of silence. This helps us remember to count in quaver beats.

THREE quavers are worth a dotted crotchet beat. Hence if you have THREE quaver rests, you can use 𝄼.

2. $\frac{2}{2}$ → looking back at the diagram, we need 2 minims to make a semibreve. **Hence, 2 means minim beats.**

The note and rest grouping in this time signature is the same as the note grouping we have learnt even though this is in minim beats.

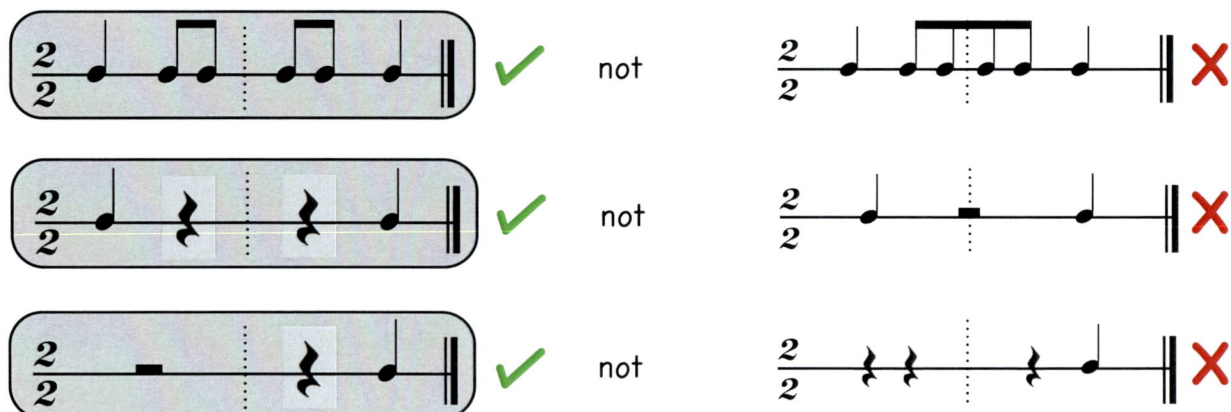

Summary of different time signatures.

$\frac{2}{2}$	$\frac{2}{4}$	$\frac{6}{8}$
2 **minim** beats in a bar	2 **crotchet** beats in a bar	6 quaver beats in a bar grouped in **dotted crotchet** beats
quavers grouped in FOURS	quavers grouped in PAIRS	quavers grouped in THREES

Complete the following bars with rests.

Write out the correct beats of each bar and join the notes with a beam to show the correct number of beats per bar.

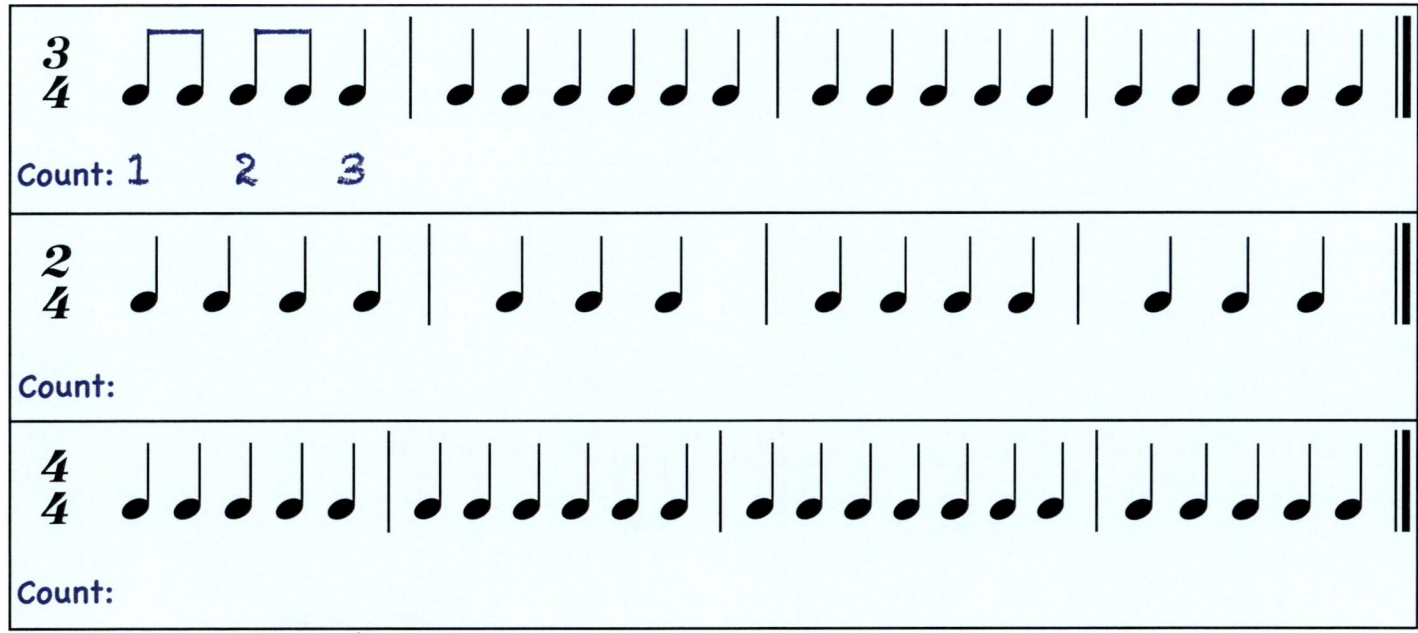

Write out the correct beats of each bar and change the values with either one of the actions below to show the correct number of beats per bar. Add...

1. a dot after the note
2. a tail or two
3. a beam
4. colour note head

Reading Rhythms

Rhythm is the most important thing in music as it defines the way a piece is to be played.

Beat vs. Rhythm
Beat is a constant pulse like a heart beat or a ticking clock.
Rhythm is a pattern of different note values where the length of each note can vary.

Rhythms can be read in a number of ways. See below for various approaches that can be used.

NOTES	FRENCH TIME NAMES	HUNGARIAN TIME NAMES	STANDARD COUNTING
♩	ta	ta	1
♫	ta te	ti ti	1 n
♬♬	ta-fa te-fe	ti-ka ti-ka	1-e n-a
♩♬	ta te-fe	ti ti-ka	1 n-a
♬♩	ta-fa te	ti-ka ti	1-e n

Below are a few rhythmic notations to practice by clapping and saying aloud the prefered rhythmic names. *Eg. ta- te, tafa tefe, etc if using the french names.* (**NOTE:** The rhythmic notation below has no note heads, therefore they are known as stick notations.)

A.
B.
C.

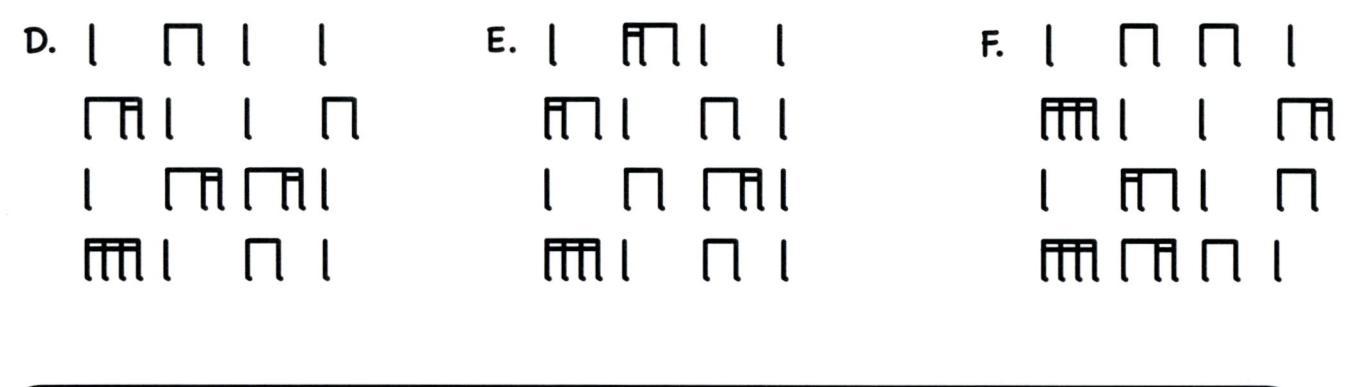

More printable rhythmic dictations are available at
www.stringstastic.com

We can also read rhythms by using words.
Each note can be repesented by a word based on the number of notes, the more notes the more syllables.

Write out as many word(s) as you know to match the rhythm given in each box below.

♩ cat slow crawl Bob	♫ co-py	♬
♫ but-ter scotch	♬ ca-ter-pil-lar	♫
♫ goose-ber-ry	♩♫	♬♫

Using the words you collected from the page before, create your own rhyme with the rhythms given below.

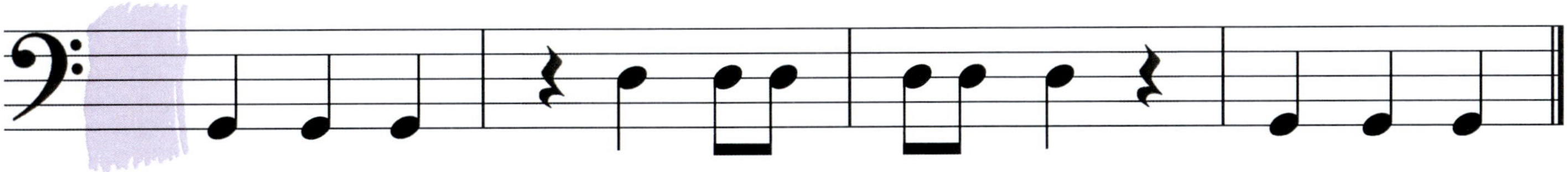

crawl Bob crawl

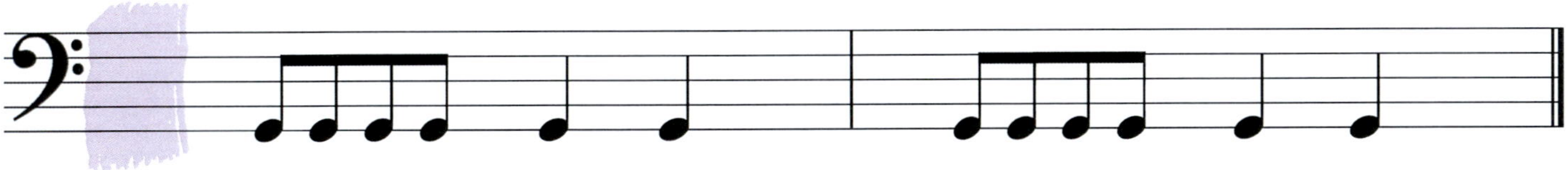

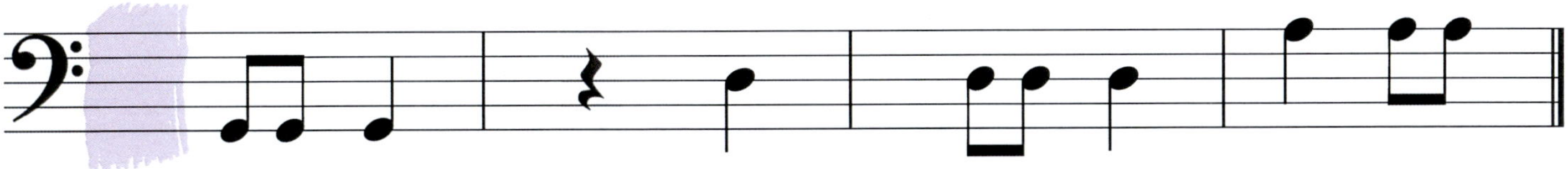

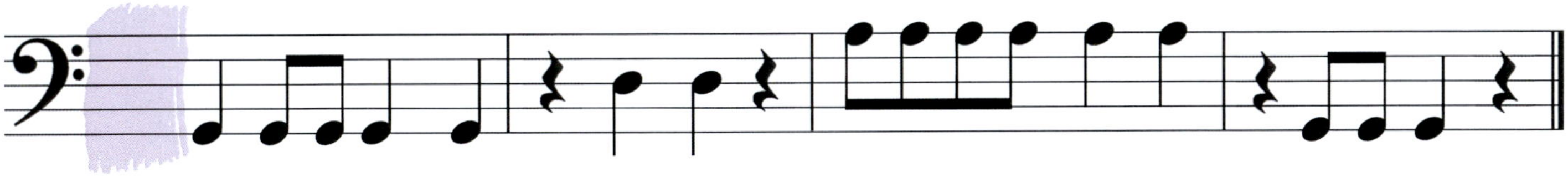

In crotchet note beat value, fill in the missing time signatures in the question above.

Now try and play the rhythm above with your cello using the words you have written down.
(Saying the words out loud while playing can help you play correctly.)

Relative Minors and Majors

Just as you have direct relatives in your family, major keys have minor keys who are relatives - think of it as your relatives that share the same surname as you do.
The major and relative minors share the same key signature.

From Level 2, we learnt that C major has no sharps or flats in its key signature. C major's relative minor key is A minor. Therefore A minor also does not have any sharps or flats in its key signature.

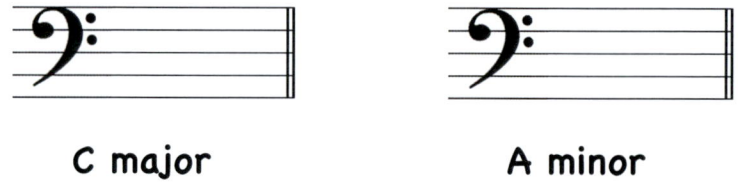

C major   A minor

Try memorising that C major is related to A minor.

There are a few ways of finding out the relative minors of the major keys. Let us look at your fingerboard and find the note A and C.

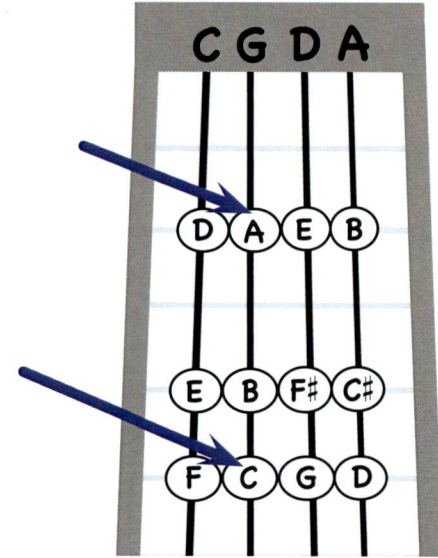

Let us look at how many steps it takes from the note C to A.

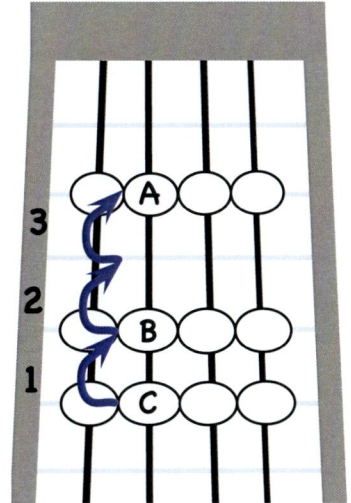

It only takes 3 steps *(3 semitones)* **back from** C to A.

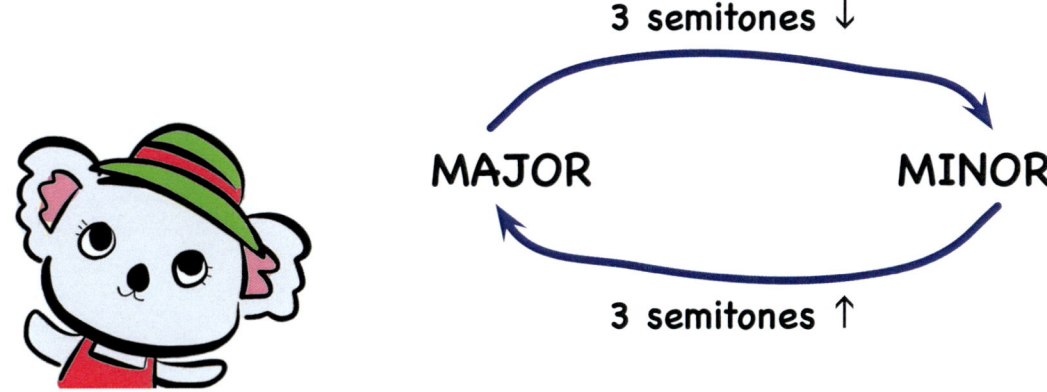

Hence the relative minors for the major scales we have learnt are as below.

C major ⟶ A minor

G major ⟶ E minor

D major ⟶ B minor

Check on the fingerboard in the previous page to see if the related minors for the major scales above are correct.

Below is how the key signature would look for each related key.

C major   A minor   G major   E minor   D major   B minor

Draw the key signature for these keys.

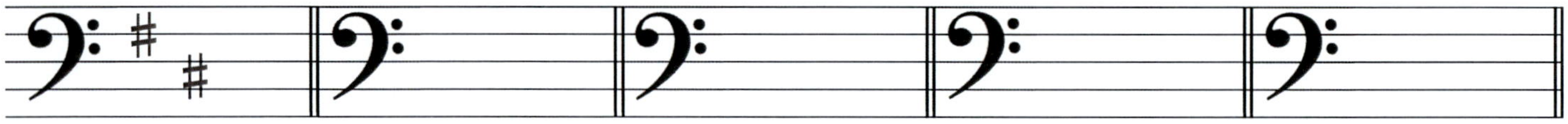

| D major | A minor | G major | B minor | E minor |

The scales and arpeggios below are missing their key signature. Using the key signatures we have learnt up till now, draw the appropriate key signature and figure out if they are in a major or minor scale.

Eg.

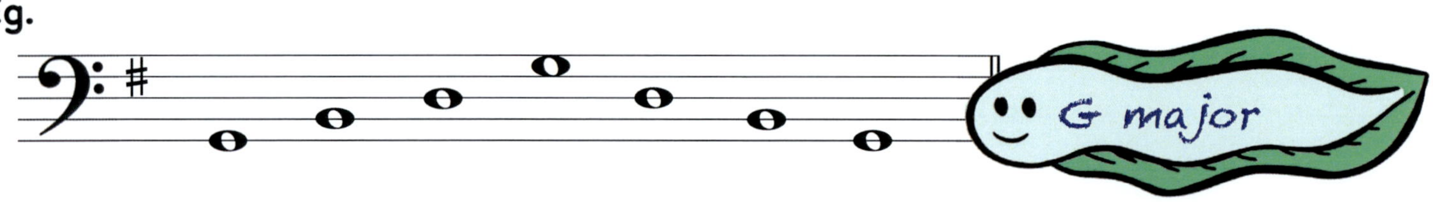

G major

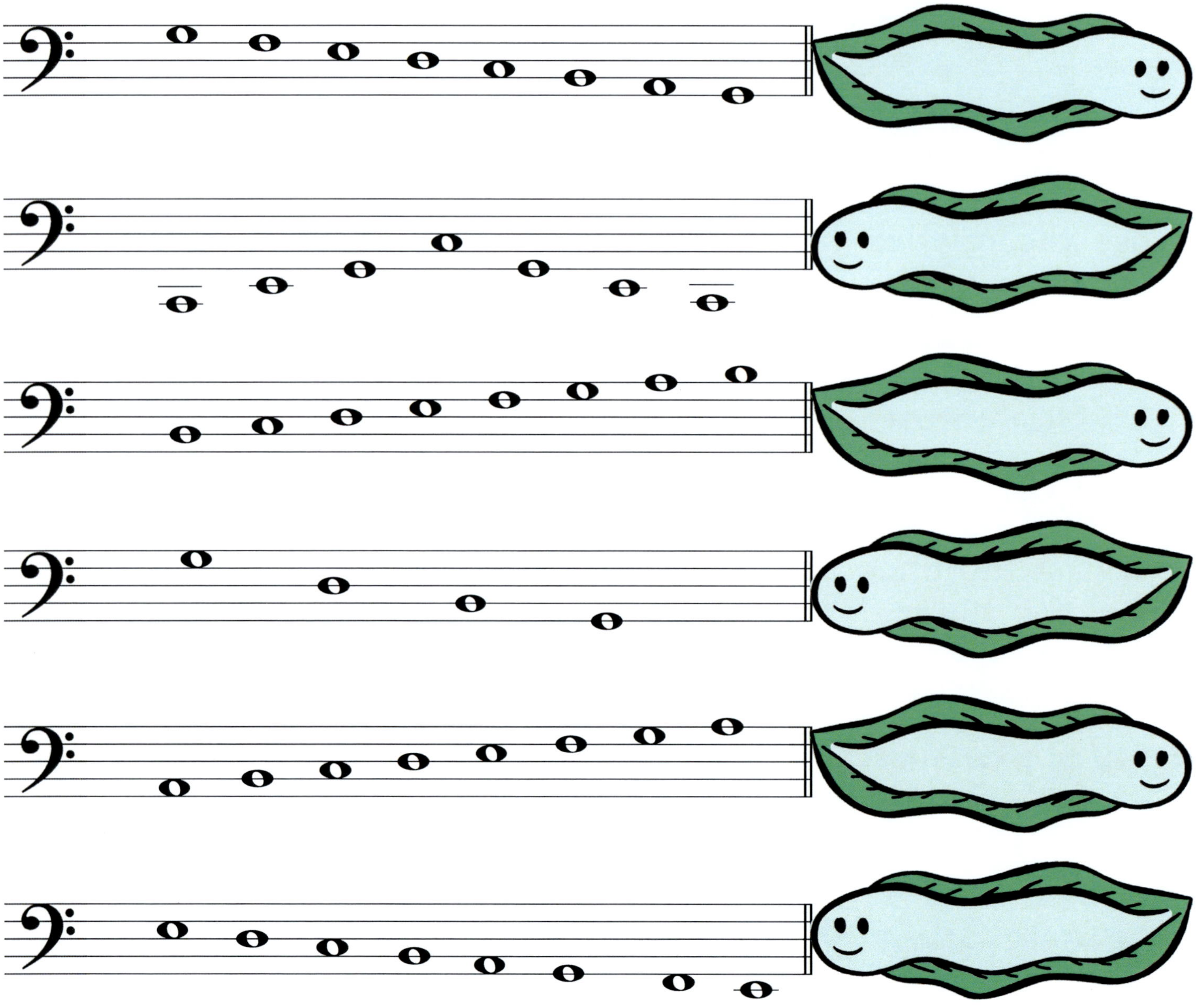

Minor Scales

The difference between a major and minor scale is that major sounds happy and minor sounds sad.

Major
Minor

There are 3 different quality types of minor scales.

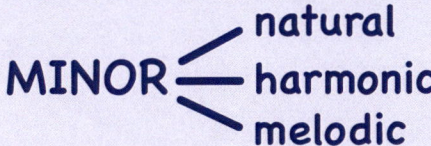

It is very easy to remember the difference between the three minor scales.

natural - normal (NO change)

Now look at the first letter of the next 2 minor scales (harmonic and melodic). How many curves does the letter have?

harmonic - 1 hump/curve = 1 change
raise the 7th note

melodic - 2 humps/curves = 2 changes
raise the 6th & 7th note going up ↑
lower the 6th & 7th note going down ↓

A natural minor

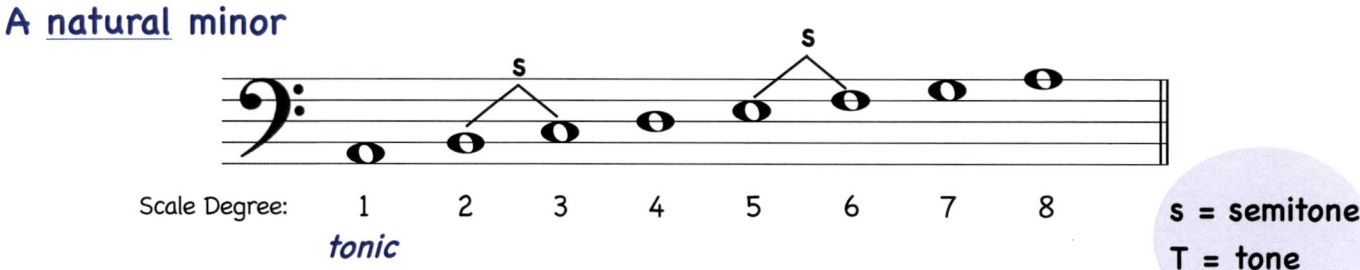

Scale Degree: 1 2 3 4 5 6 7 8
tonic

s = semitone
T = tone

The tone-semitone pattern of any natural minor scale is as below,

T - s - T - T - s - T - T

Between which scale degree numbers are the semitones?

____-____ and ____-____

Scale degree is another way of labelling the notes by using numbers. It starts with the first note of the scale being number 1. The bigger the number, the higher the note.

A harmonic minor

Scale Degree: 1 2 3 4 5 6 7 8
tonic

raise the 7th note ↑
(there is always a (tone + semitone) pattern in a harmonic scale)
between the 6th & 7th degrees

The tone-semitone pattern of any harmonic minor scale is as below,

T - s - T - T - s - T and a half - s

Between which scale degree numbers are the semitones?

____-____ , ____-____ and ____-____

How many types of minor scales are there?

Name all the different quality types of minor scales available.

_____

_____

_____

Change these natural minors into harmonic minors.
(HINT: Raise the 7th degree.)

A harmonic minor

(REMINDER: Count the scale degree from the lowest note.)

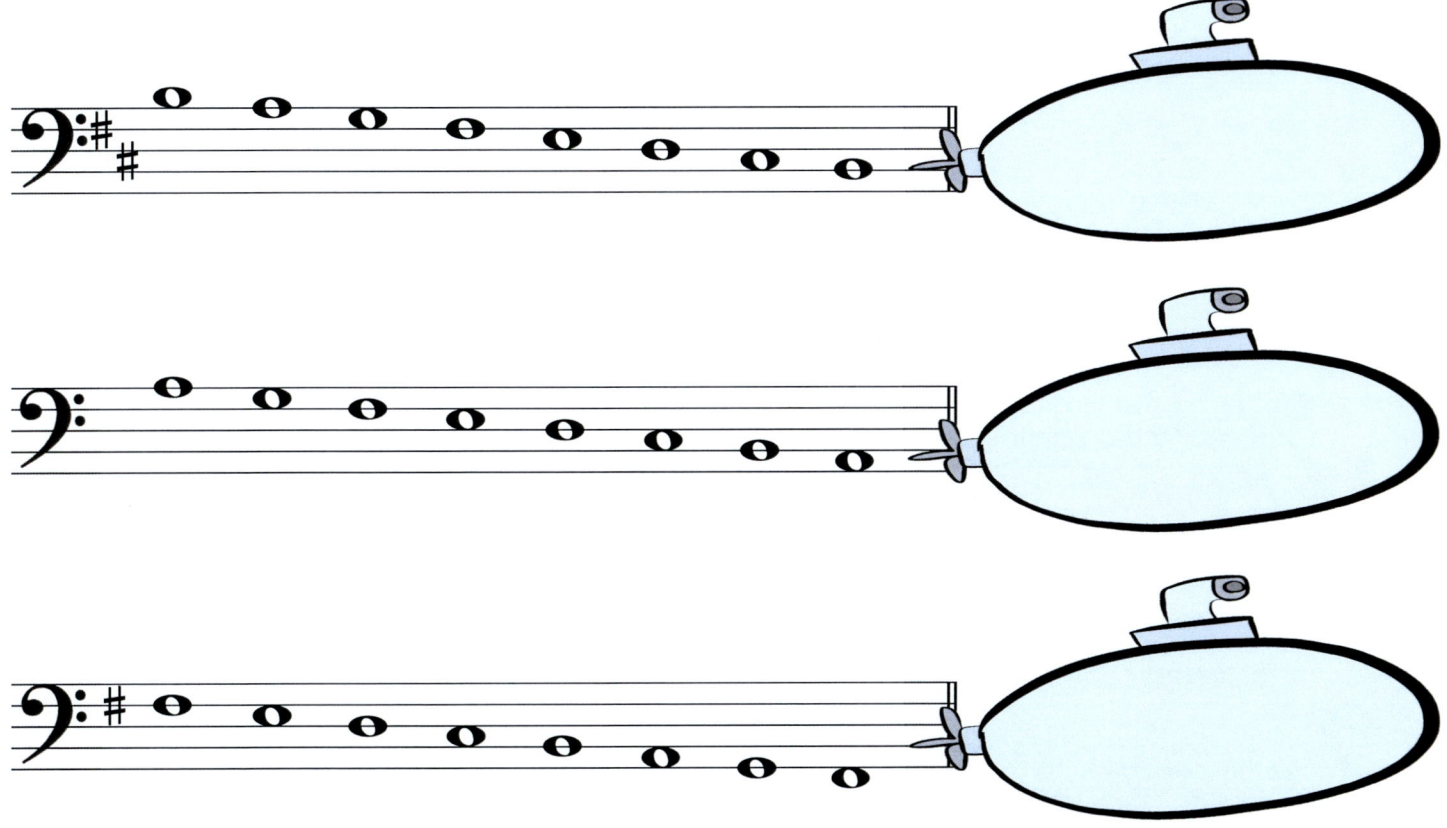

Name the scales above.

Now try playing these harmonic scales on your cello.

Lastly let us see what a melodic minor scale looks like.

A melodic minor

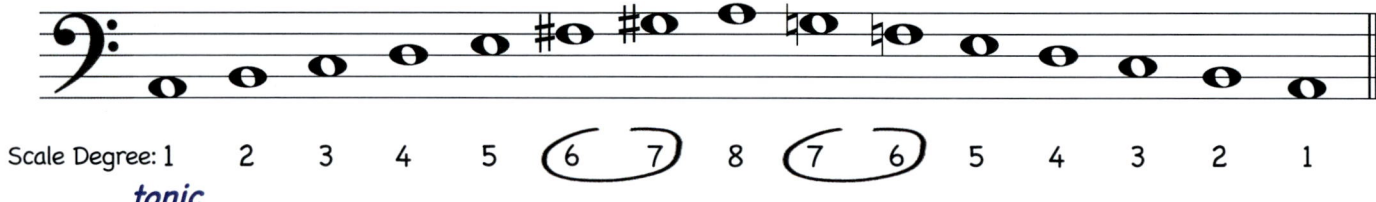

Scale Degree: 1 2 3 4 5 (6 7) 8 (7 6) 5 4 3 2 1
tonic

raise the 6th & 7th note going up ↑
lower the 6th & 7th note going down ↓

In minims, write a ONE octave minor scale in an ascending and descending order. (REMINDER: Sometimes you need to add accidentals.)

B harmonic minor

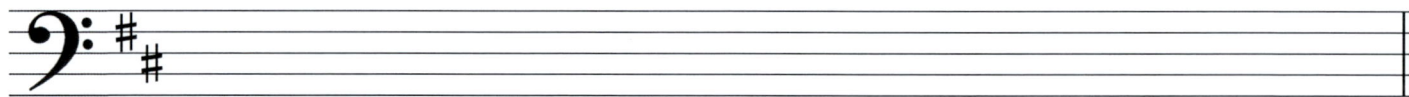

A natural minor

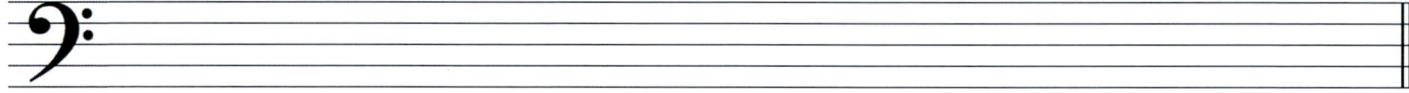

E natural minor

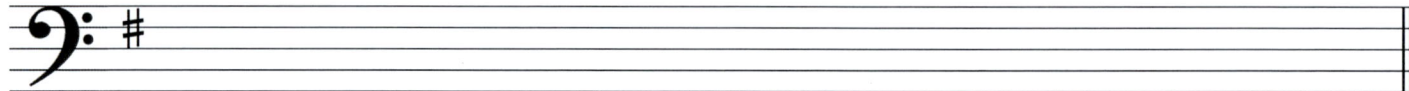

E harmonic minor

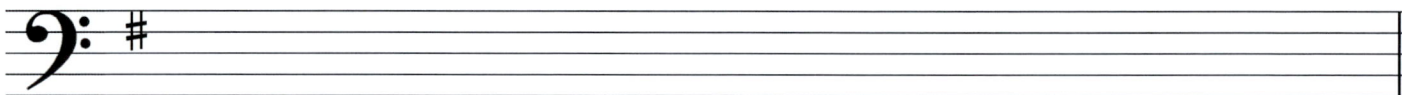

B melodic minor

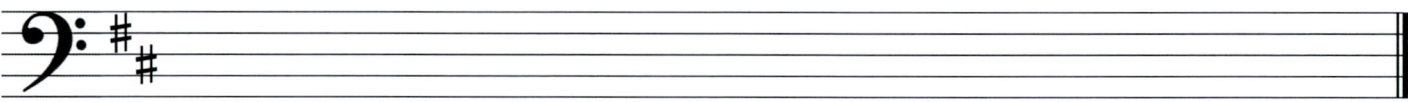

Now try playing these scales on your cello.
Can you hear the difference between the natural, harmonic and melodic minor scales?

B natural minor

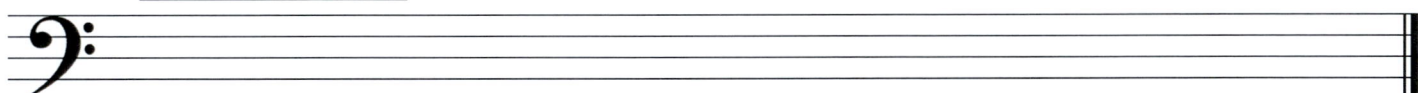

A harmonic minor

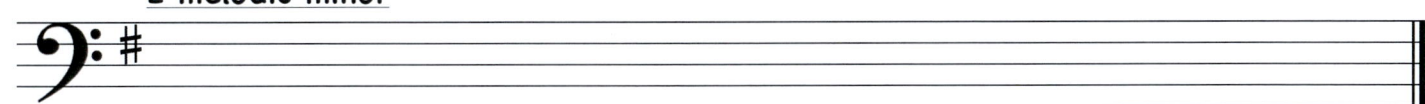

E melodic minor

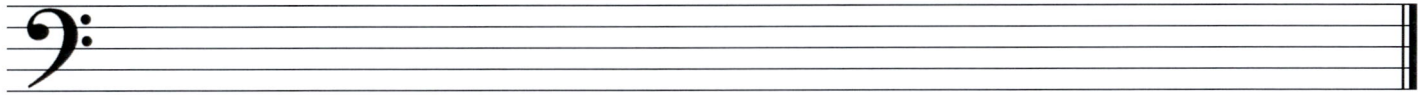

A melodic minor

On pages 23 through to 25, number the scale degrees and add slurs to show where the semitones are and mark them with an 's'.

How many semitones are there in a natural minor scale?

How many semitones are there in a harmonic minor scale?

On which scale degree in a harmonic scale would you find the two notes which are a <u>tone and a half</u>?

Minor Arpeggios

Remember from Level 2, <u>arpeggios</u> are notes of a chord played one after another. We use the 1st, 3rd and 5th notes of a scale. We also include the 8th note.

Eg.

A minor

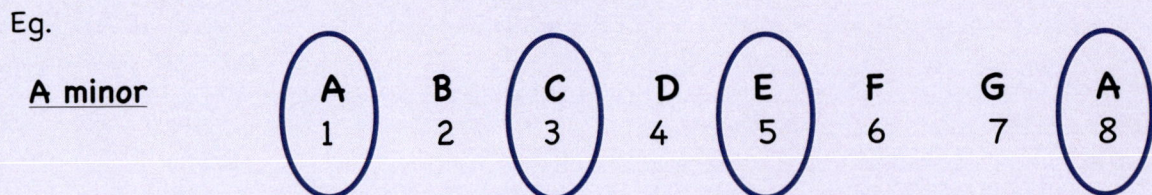

Circle the notes of the arpeggio of these scales below.

B minor

B   C#   D   E   F#   G   A   B

E minor

E   F#   G   A   B   C   D   E

Draw the arpeggio from these scales (using crotchet notes) **in an <u>ascending</u> and <u>descending</u> order.**

B minor

A minor

E minor

In semibreve notes, draw the same arpeggio scales in a descending and ascending order.

A minor

B minor

E minor

Now draw these scales (using minim notes) **in an ascending and descending order.**

A melodic minor

B melodic minor

E melodic minor

**Now try playing these scales on your cello.
Can you play these scales by memory? Let us try...**

Labelling Scales and Arpeggios

Label the scales and arpeggios below, then their movement.
(**NOTE:** The scales and arpeggios below are written with and without key signatures.)

What have we learnt so far?

Fill in the missing spaces on note values.

NOTE NAME	NOTE	NOTE VALUE
se_i_ua_er	♪	1/4
_e_iqu_ver re_t		
cro_c_e_		
q_av_r		
do__ed c_otc_et		

Tommy just had his birthday party and has too many birthday cupcakes left over. How many cupcakes did Tommy's friends take home?

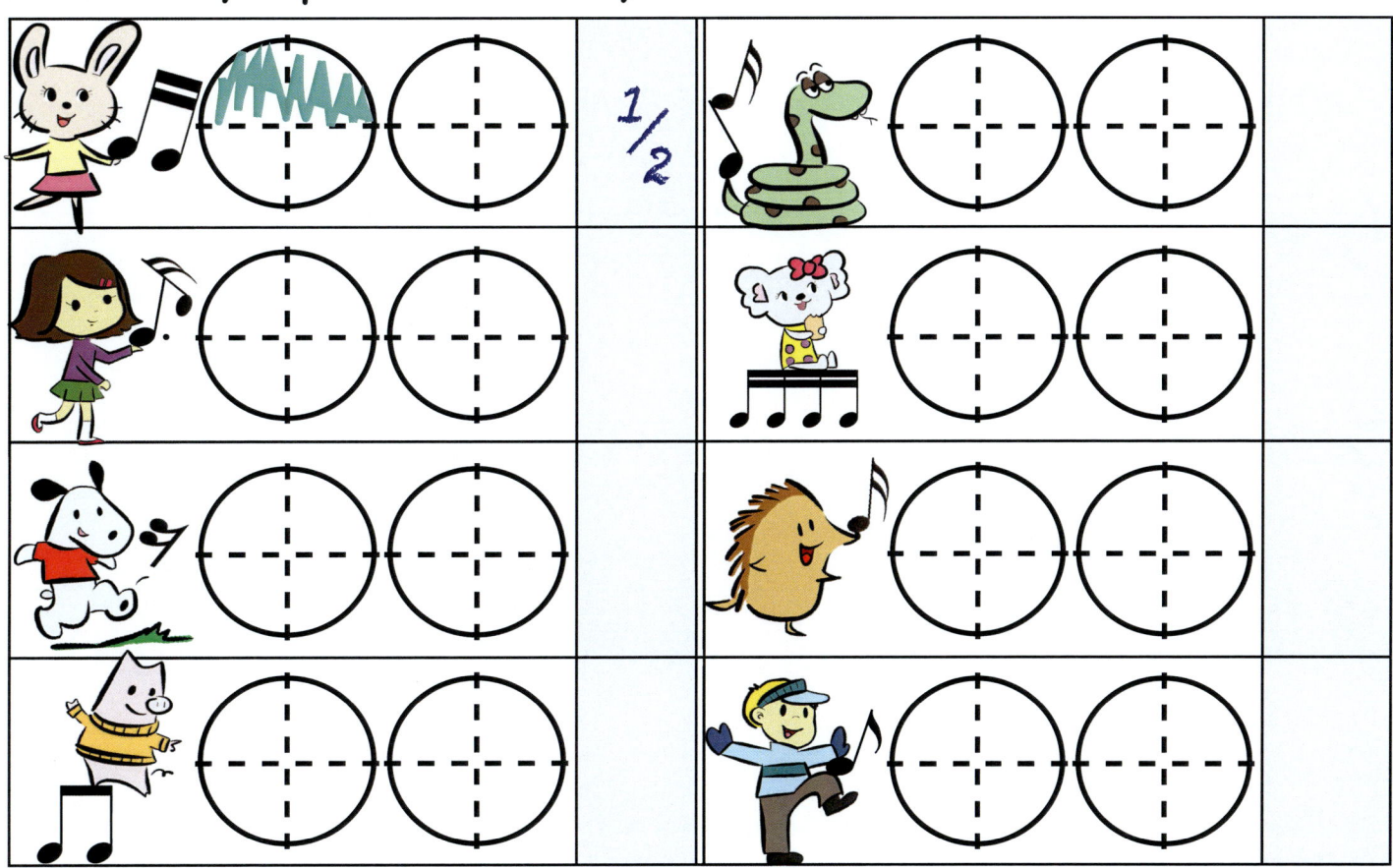

Clap and say the rhythms out loud.
Work out how many beats there are in each bar and write out the correct time signature.

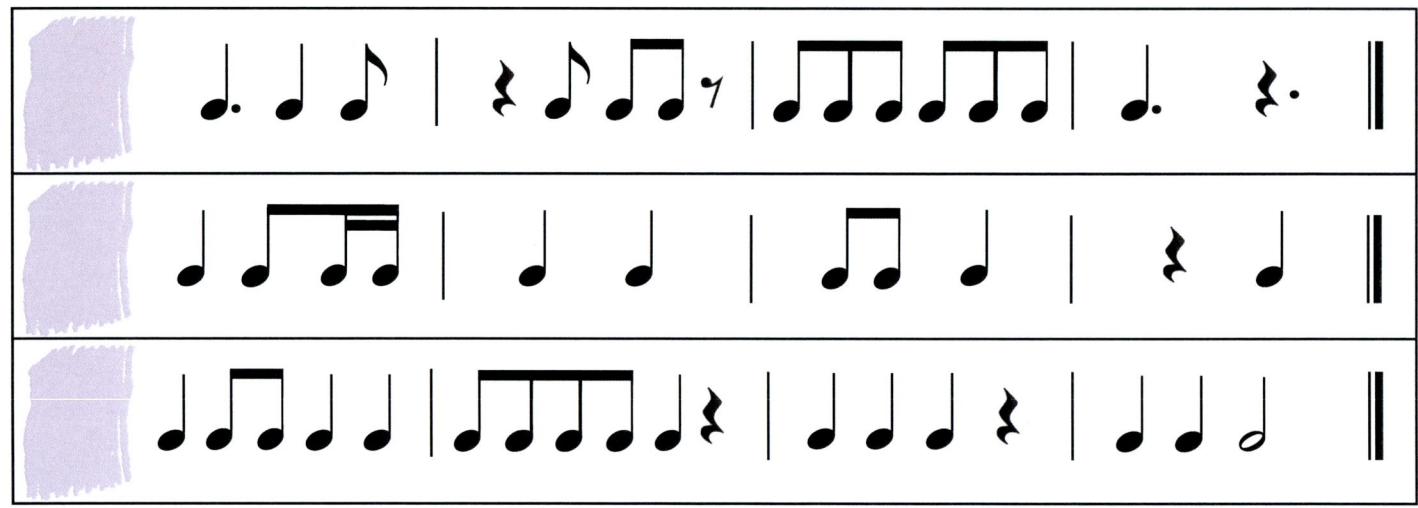

How many types of minor scales are there?

Name all the different quality types of minor scales available.

_____

_____

_____

Draw out the 3 different quality types of E minor scales in an ascending and descending order using semibreves.

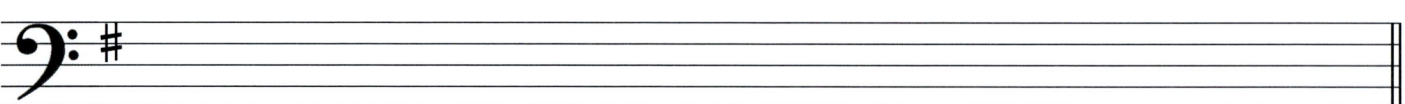

Label the semitones in the exercise above with a slur.

Sequences

A <u>sequence</u> is a melodic pattern that is repeated starting on a different note each time, either moving the whole pattern upwards or downwards. (REMINDER: Take care of the stem direction.)

Eg.

Draw a bracket (⌐⌐) over each step of the sequence.

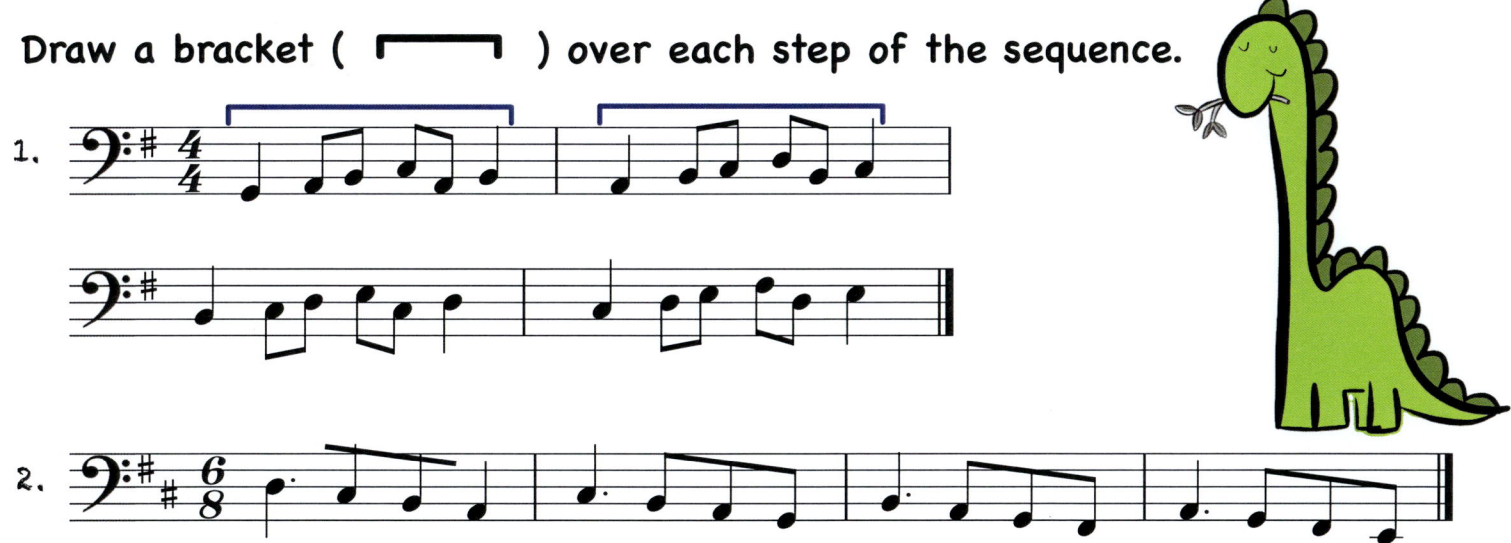

Make a sequence by repeating it twice, one note <u>higher</u> each time using the tune given.

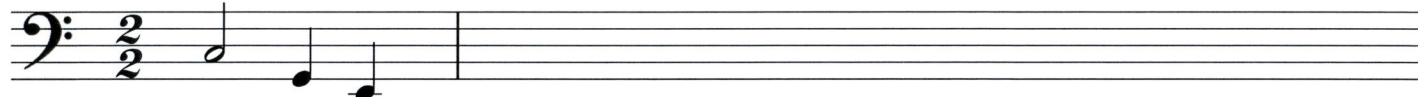

Make a sequence by repeating it twice, one note <u>lower</u> each time using the tune given.

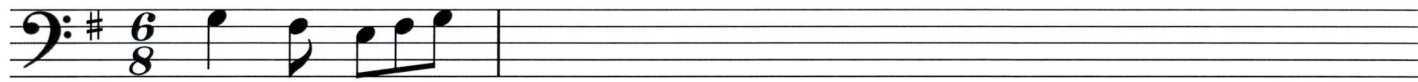

Now try playing these sequences on your cello.
Can you hear how the tune moves?

Ostinato

An <u>ostinato</u> is a repeated rhythmic and pitch pattern.
 Eg.

Draw 3 more ostinato patterns.

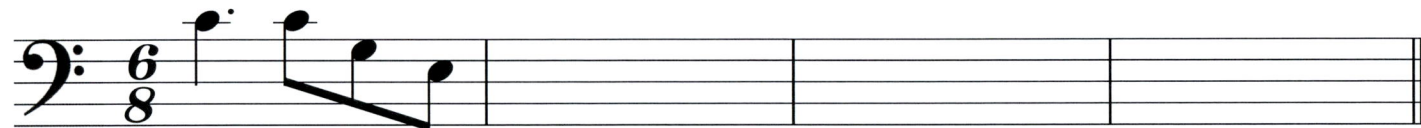

Ostinato vs. Sequence
Ostinato is a repeated rhythmic pattern with the same notes. Sequence is a repeated rhythmic and pitch pattern. It maintains the tune but moves the whole tune up or down.

Now try playing these ostinato pattern on your cello. Can you hear the difference between ostinato and sequence?

Italian Terms

Expression Marking
Expression Marking tells a player in what kind of mood to play the music. They are written below the music.

dolce - sweetly
cantabile - in a singing style
espressivo - expressively
grazioso - gracefully
leggiero - lightly
molto - very

> Sometimes the way we remember meanings of terms is by looking at the first few letters of the music term. It is usually close to the english definition.

Tempo Marking
Tempo Marking tells a player in which speed to play the music.

Let us revise what we have learnt in Level 1 and 2 on Tempo.
Fill in the blanks where needed.

Vivace - fast and lively

Allegro -

Allegretto - quite fast (but slower than Allegro)

Moderato -

Andante -

Adagio -

Lento - slowly
piu mosso - slower (less speed)
meno mosso - faster (more speed)
simile - similar

Figure out the italian terms for the meanings below.

1. Moderate speed.
2. When you hold a note longer then its value.
3. Gradually slowing down.
4. Fast.
5. Finish or the end.
6. Slow speed.
7. Similar.
8. Short and detached.
9. Loud.
10. Sweetly.
11. Repeated pitch and rhythmic pattern.
12. Majestically.
13. Smoothly.
14. Gradually getting softer.
15. Animated.
16. In a singing style.
17. Go back to the beginning.
18. Type of articulation.

Composition

There are many ways of composing music.

In Level 3, we learn how to write short tunes by using the first FIVE notes of a given scale to a given rhythm.

TIP: Start and end the tune using the FIRST note of the scale.

Eg. B minor

The first 5 notes for B minor are **B C♯ D E F♯**.
Below is one way we can write a tune using these notes.

Write a tune using the first FIVE notes of a given scale and rhythm.
(REMINDER: Write in the key and time signature.)

C major

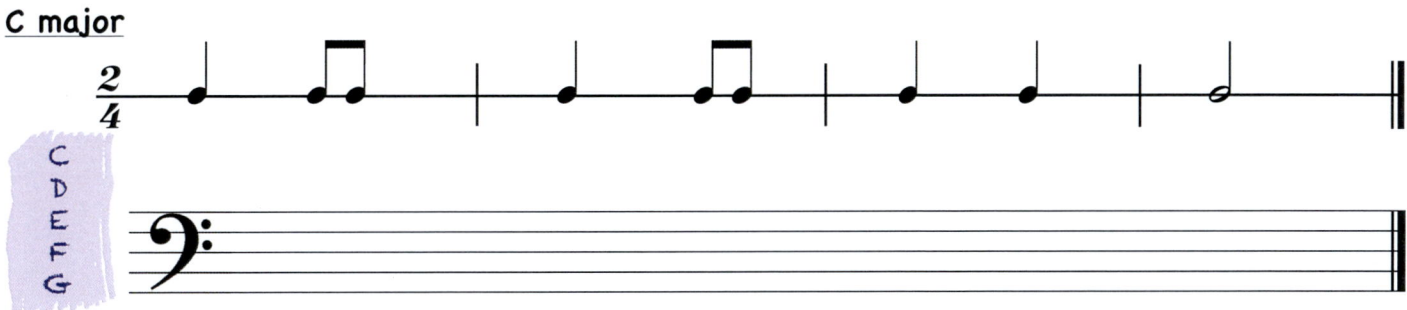

A minor

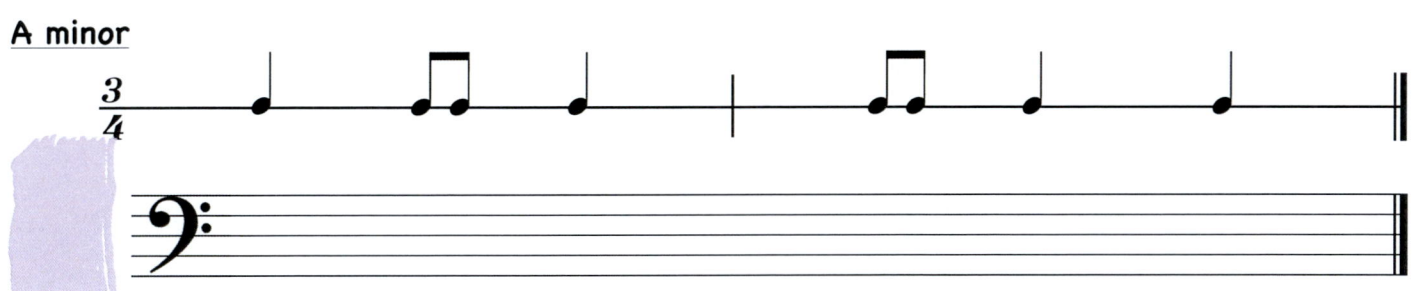

Now try playing these compositions which you have just written. Careful of the accidentals used.
Where do you lower your first and second finger in these short tunes?

Anacrusis

An anacrusis is a note or a series of notes that comes before the first full bar. It can also be referred to as an upbeat.

As string players, we use an up-bow (∨) for a single up-beat note. This means that a down-bow (⊓) occurs on the first beat of the bar.

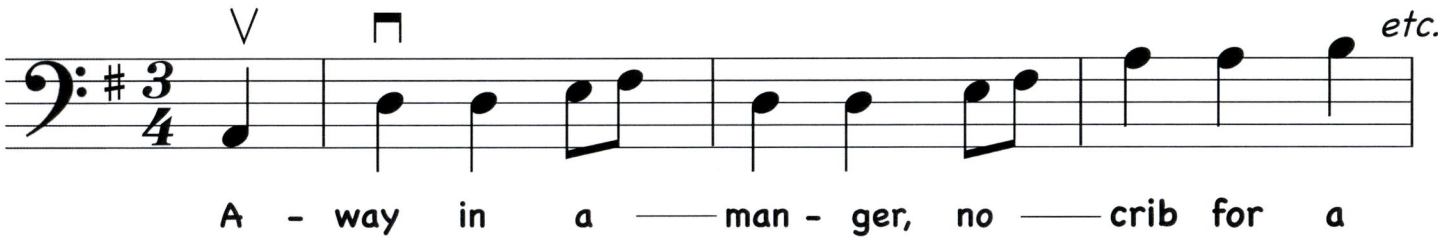

When you sing these tunes, notice how you emphasise more on the underlined words.

a- <u>MAZ</u>- ing   NOT <u>A</u>-maz-ing   NOT a-maz-<u>ING</u>

a- <u>WAY</u>   NOT <u>A</u>-way

Occasionally when you have more than one upbeat note, they do not always start with the up-bow.

(**REMINDER:** The first beat of the first full bar always starts with a down bow (⊓)).

As shown below,

When a piece begins on an upbeat, the final bar has fewer beats than usual. The amount of beats in the anacrusis is taken out of the last bar to even out the difference.

The following rhythms begin with an anacrusis, but the note value on the last bar is **INCORRECT** (too many beats). Rewrite the rhythm with the correct note value on the last bar.

Half Position

Shifting
Shifting refers to the whole left hand moving smoothly up or down the fingerboard (like an elevator) to play notes in different positions on the fingerboard.
When we first started learning the cello, our 1st finger is placed on the 1st line. This is called the first position (the 1st finger on the first line of the fingering strip).

Different positions
A few new positions that need to be learnt. By now we should be 'experts' on the first position (original position).
In order to identify the other positions depends on where the first finger is placed. If the first finger is moved to the 2nd strip on the fingering board, you will be in 2nd position. If the 1st finger is moved to the 3rd line, you will be in 3rd position and so on.

Benefits:
- gain more notes on each string
- more possibilities for fingerings to help play any tune
- help improve smooth playing of fast passages

Requirements:
- thumb is not left behind when fingers move
- control of finger spacing (tone and semitone)
- standing fingertip position enabling smaller spacing
- elbow moves

We use Roman Numerals to mark the different positions which is shown below,

> I - First Position
> II - Second Position
> III - Third Position
> IV - Fourth Position
> V - Fifth Position
> etc.

In Level 3 cello, we will only touch base on the half position and not the other ones. The lowest note on any string is achieved by either using backward extension from the first position or by moving all four fingers lower by one semitone.

Unlike the violin and the viola, we use the half position for a more comfortable way of playing.

Play these scales and figure out if you will be using the normal position, backward or forward extension? (You can use more than one position.)

normal position

We have not learnt some of the scales written above, however, after playing them, could you tell if they were a major or minor scale?

Forward Extension

Remember how we learnt backward extension in Level 2 cello? All the finger position is the same except the 1st finger. In Level 3 cello, we look at the forward extension.

Forward extension is where the first finger is the only finger that stays in place while the other fingers stretch forward. Below is an example of how the backward and forward extension looks like compared to the normal position.

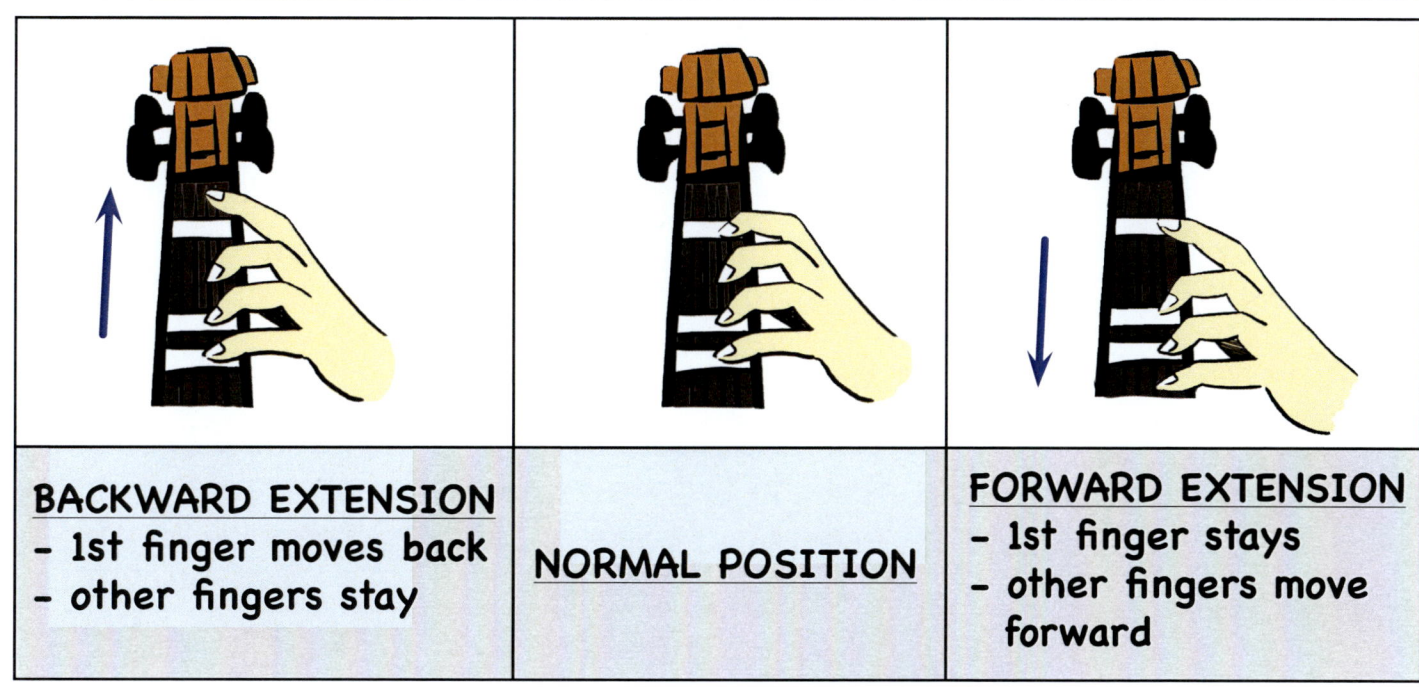

BACKWARD EXTENSION
- 1st finger moves back
- other fingers stay

NORMAL POSITION

FORWARD EXTENSION
- 1st finger stays
- other fingers move forward

Raise the pitch and name all the notes which were originally on the 3rd line a semitone forward.

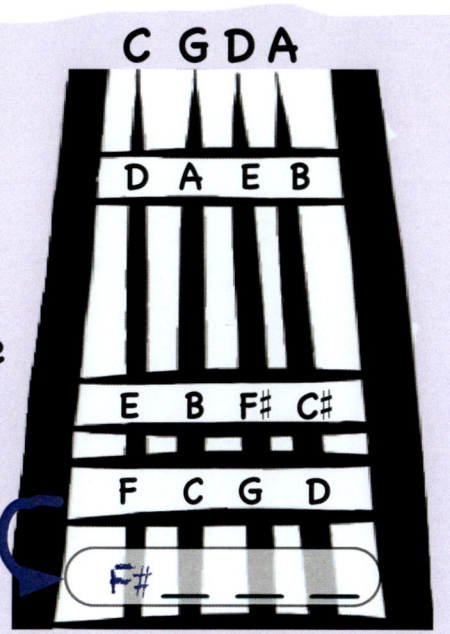

Last Revision

1. Cross out the answers which are incorrect.

leggiero	lightly	~~smoothly~~
Vivace	viper	fast and lively
grazioso	gorilla	gracefully
A minor	has ONE sharp	has no sharps or flats
ostinato	repeated pitch and rhythmic pattern	repeated rhythmic pattern

2. Write a tune using the first FIVE notes of a given scale and rhythm.
   (**REMINDER:** Write in the key signature and time signature.)

3. Draw the key signature of these minor keys.

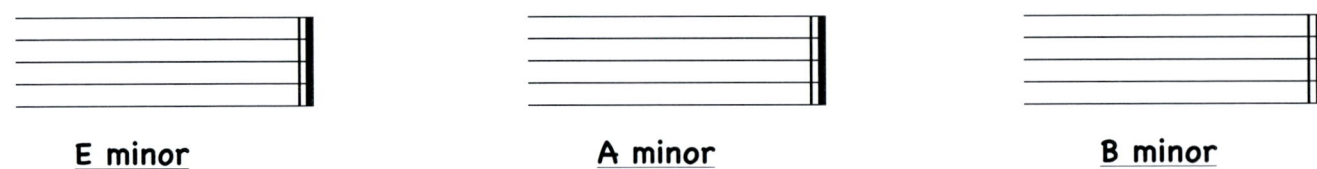

E minor   A minor   B minor

4. **Write out the D harmonic scale using the correct key signature.**
   - draw the bass clef
   - one octave ascending only
   - use semibreve notes
   - complete the scale with a double bar line

5. **Help Suzie decorate the Christmas tree using the different coloured ornaments mentioned accordingly.**

| ½ count | 1 count | 2 counts | 3 counts |
| yellow | red | blue | orange |

6. **What do these time signatures mean?**

   3/4 _3 crotchet beats in a bar_

   2/2 _____

   6/8 _____

44

Name: _____ Date: _____

Test

TOTAL MARKS: _____/100

1. **Name these notes.** (**REMINDER**: Use capital letters.) _____/9

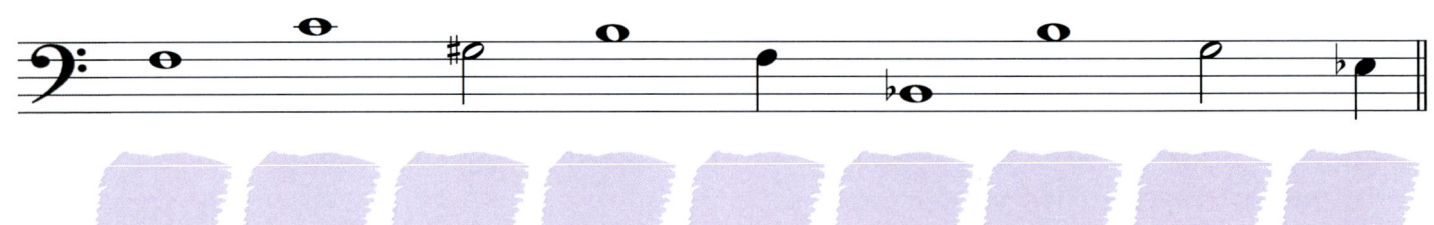

2. In first position, write out the correct fingering above the notes in question 1. _____/9

3. Match the major and minor keys to its correct key signature.

   _____/6

   C major

   D major

   G major

   B minor

   A minor

   E minor

4. What are the definitions of these words. _____/8

   A. *grazioso*

   B. *dolce*

   C. *cantabile*

   D. *espressivo*

5. Write out these scales using the correct key signature. _____/20

E harmonic minor
- Draw the bass clef
- One octave descending only
- Use crotchet notes
- Complete the scale with a double bar line

A melodic minor
- Draw the bass clef
- One octave in an ascending and descending order
- Use minim notes
- Complete the scale with a double bar line

D major arpeggio
- Draw the bass clef
- One octave in an ascending and descending order
- Use semibreve notes
- Complete the scale with a double bar line

B minor arpeggio
- Draw the bass clef
- One octave in a descending and ascending order
- Use quaver notes in pairs
- Complete the scale with a double bar line

6. **Using the key signature of G major, write a tune using the first FIVE notes of the scale.** _____/6

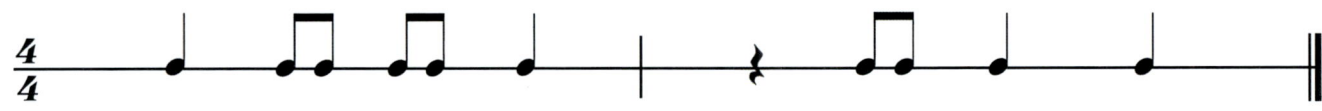

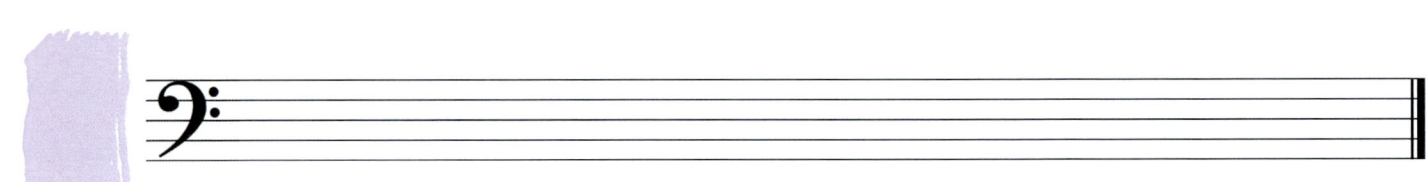

7. **Tick the correct definition of these words below.** _____/2

   A. An ostinato is a ......
   - ○ repeated balancing act
   - ○ repeated rhythmic pattern but moves up or down by one note each time
   - ○ repeated rhythmic and pitch pattern

   B. Sequence is a ......
   - ○ repeated balancing act
   - ○ repeated rhythmic pattern but moves up or down by one note each time
   - ○ repeated rhythmic and pitch pattern

8. **Fill in the blanks.** _____/30

	DYNAMIC or TEMPO	Written ABOVE or BELOW the music	DEFINITION
Vivace			
crescendo			
Adagio			
meno mosso			
mezzo forte			

9. Answer the questions below. ____/4

A. How many ♪'s are in a ♩ ?

B. How many pairs of ♫'s are in a 𝅗𝅥 ?

C. How many ♪'s are in a ♩ ?

D. How many ♪'s are in a 𝅗𝅥 ?

10. How many counts should the last note be in the rhythm given below? ____/2

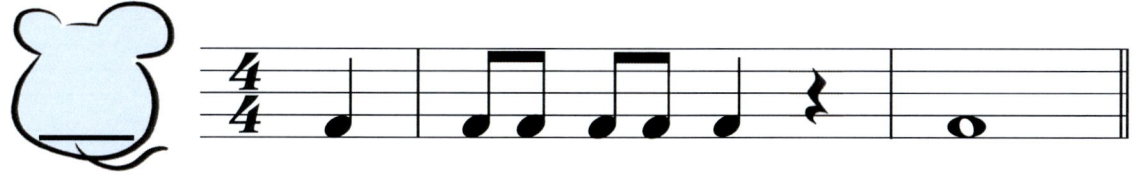

11. Circle the anacrusis on the rhythm in question 10. ____/2

12. Write in the bow marking on the first note on question 10. ____/2